Mini
Pusheen™
COLORING BOOK

Claire Belton

GALLERY BOOKS

New York London Toronto Sydney New Delhi

GALLERY BOOKS

An Imprint of Simon & Schuster, Inc.
1230 Avenue of the Americas
New York, NY 10020

Copyright © 2016 by Pusheen Corp.
This is an abridged edition of *Pusheen Coloring Book*

This Gallery Books trade paperback edition May 2019

GALLERY BOOKS and colophon are registered trademarks of Simon & Schuster, Inc.

For information about special discounts for bulk purchases,
please contact Simon & Schuster Special Sales at 1-866-506-1949
or business@simonandschuster.com.

The Simon & Schuster Speakers Bureau can bring authors to your live event.
For more information or to book an event, contact the Simon & Schuster Speakers Bureau
at 1-866-248-3049 or visit our website at www.simonspeakers.com.

Manufactured in the United States of America

10

ISBN 978-1-5011-8097-2

My Beach Essentials

Donuts

Pizza

Cake

Bacon

Pusheen's guide to
being fancy

Not fancy

Kind of fancy?

Fancy

Super fancy

I love kitties!

Discover more from Pusheen!

75767